IMAGES
of America

OCRACOKE

The old homestead sits quietly behind a sprawling live oak on a sandy lane. In the distance is the lighthouse, built in 1823. Electrical poles to the left indicate that progress has reached the island, as Ocracoke was electrified in 1938. Tire tracks signify growth, as the automobile brought a larger ferry service, paved roads, and more residents and tourists. (Courtesy of the State Archives of North Carolina.)

ON THE COVER: Two musicians pose outside of the Pamlico Inn prior to its destruction in the 1944 hurricane. Evidence of damage from a gas tank explosion on New Year's Eve 1929 can be seen on the bulkhead. Musicians flocked to the inn to play on Saturday nights, and tourists and locals alike joined in the revelry. (Courtesy of the Outer Banks History Center, Aycock Brown Collection.)

IMAGES
of America

OCRACOKE

Jeanie Owens

ARCADIA
PUBLISHING

Published by Arcadia Publishing
Charleston, South Carolina

Printed in the United States of America

Library of Congress Control Number: 2017949968

For all general information, please contact Arcadia Publishing:
Telephone 843-853-2070
Fax 843-853-0044
E-mail sales@arcadiapublishing.com
For customer service and orders:
Toll-Free 1-888-313-2665

Visit us on the Internet at www.arcadiapublishing.com

To Annelise and Eli, you are loved beyond words.
To Jeramy, you are my everything.
To my mom and our family, I love you more.
To the children of Ocracoke, you are in my soul.

CONTENTS

ACKNOWLEDGMENTS

Since 1992, the Ocracoke Preservation Society (OPS) museum has operated out of the David Williams home. Upstairs is a quaint library filled with photographs and resources where I spent my summer learning about the village I love. Special thanks go to the staff and volunteers at OPS, including Andrea Powers and former employees Allison O'Neal and Rachel King, for their patience, time, and use of their scanner. This book is only possible because of their kindness. I wish to extend my gratitude to the staffs of the Outer Banks History Center, the North Carolina State Archives, the Wilson Library at UNC–Chapel Hill, and the Mariners' Museum for allowing me to use their archived photographs.

My heartfelt gratitude goes to the Ocracokers who guided me through my research. I wish to thank Chester Lynn, who inspired me to keep researching and let me use his priceless images. I so enjoyed the numerous visits we had together. My appreciation goes to Sue and Vince O'Neal for sharing resources with me and for being my go-to couple when I needed pictures identified. They allowed me to take photographs off their restaurant wall and interrupt an Orioles game. My thanks and admiration go to Philip Howard for sharing his photographs and for his two informative websites: his newsletter www.villagecraftsmen.com/ocracoke-newsletter and his blog villagecraftsmen.blogspot.com. He does not realize how many countless hours I spent reading his words. A special thanks is extended to Alton Ballance, whose definitive work, *Ocracokers*, guided me through Ocracoke's past and let me walk in the footsteps of a local. A special tribute goes to Earl O'Neal, whose passing saddened us all; his wisdom lives on through his works. I want to thank Della Gaskill, whose book is a tender reflection of a beautiful life.

A special thank-you goes to my title manager, Caitrin Cunningham, for her support and guidance. Thanks go to the staff of Ocracoke School, of which I am so honored to be a part. I wish to extend heartfelt appreciation and love go to my partner, Jeramy, for being patient during this process. Finally, a big thank-you and love to my children, Annelise and Eli, for encouraging me to attain my goal. They are my constant examples of determination and perseverance.

The images in this volume appear courtesy of the Ocracoke Preservation Society (OPS), the Outer Banks History Center (OBHC), the State Archives of North Carolina (SANC), the Mariners' Museum (MM), the Louis Round Wilson Library Special Collections at UNC–Chapel Hill (WLUNC), Chester Lynn, Vince O'Neal, and Philip Howard.

INTRODUCTION

Ocracoke is a 16-mile-long island at the end of the Outer Banks of North Carolina, accessible only by ferry, private plane, or boat. Ocracoke is the name of both an island and an inlet. The village itself is four square miles. Research found in Alton Ballance's book, *Ocracokers*, suggests that Ocracoke was first formed around 17,000 years ago at the end of the Ice Age. It may have been located 25 miles offshore on the edge of the continental shelf. With rising sea levels, Ocracoke migrated toward the mainland due to the ocean current and the predominantly southwesterly winds that cause the sand to migrate westward and probably ended up where it is today about 3,000 to 4,000 years ago.

It is believed that Native Americans did not settle on Ocracoke. Instead, the area was used as a seasonal hunting and fishing ground. The first known European visitors to the island arrived in 1580s, when Sir Richard Grenville grounded the *Tiger* near the inlet. The explorers named the island the Native American name Wococon. Legend has it that is it is from this word that the name Ocracoke evolved. The general assembly established pilots on Ocracoke in 1715 to help ships navigate the dangerous shoals. Ocracoke Inlet was the primary water route for commerce from ports on the mainland.

Many tales come out of Ocracoke's history, including that of the infamous Blackbeard. Because the shallow water made for an easy escape from the more cumbersome Royal Navy ships, Ocracoke became a favorite hideout for pirates. Blackbeard sailed the *Adventure* into Ocracoke and began plundering ships in the Atlantic and Pamlico Sound. In the fall of 1718, pirates gathered on Ocracoke, including Charles Vane, Calico Jack Rackham, Robert Deal, Israel Hands, and Blackbeard. Virginia colonial governor Alexander Spotswood was not pleased with this. Nor did he trust the North Carolina governor, Charles Eden, who seems to have befriended Blackbeard. Spotswood enlisted two Royal Navy men, one of whom was Lt. Robert Maynard. They reached Ocracoke Inlet on November 21. Blackbeard died after a fierce battle.

Soon after Blackbeard's death, John Lovick, who had been secretary of the colony, received the island of "Occacock" in a grant from the Lords Proprietors. In 1733, Richard Sanderson of Perquimans was given the island, and upon his death, the island went to his son, Richard. In 1759, the younger Sanderson sold the island to William Howard. Howard was the fourth and final colonial owner. John Williams purchased half of the island from Howard for 52 pounds, 10 shillings on September 26, 1759. Upon his death, Williams willed his portion to his children.

Spanish privateers took possession of Ocracoke Inlet in 1747. Villagers were killed, ships burned, and livestock slaughtered. The villagers pleaded with the colonial assembly to build a fort. They were promised one, but it never came. On September 3, 1750, the islanders took revenge against the Spanish. The *Nuestra Señora Guadalupe* was caught in the inlet carrying a million pieces of eight. The captain asked the villagers for protection, but remembering the carnage of 1747, the villagers threatened instead to pillage the ship. The Spanish put half of their money on a passing ship that sailed away with the fortune. Some say this was the catalyst for Robert Louis Stevenson's *Treasure Island*.

During the Revolutionary War, Ocracoke Inlet was vital to the Patriot cause. The inlet served as the supply route to the mainland. A Revolutionary fort was constructed on the Portsmouth side of the Ocracoke Inlet in 1777. The British had closed Cape Fear and the Chesapeake Bay. Merchants on the mainland sent ships with cargos of tobacco and pork through the Ocracoke Inlet. In return, the Patriots received gunpowder, ammunition, salt, and clothes. Some of these supplies found their way to George Washington at Valley Forge.

By the first census in 1790, there were 135 whites, two free persons of color, and 23 slaves living on Ocracoke. Nine family names appear: Bragg, Garrish, Gaskins, Howard, Jackson, Neale/O'Neal, Salter, Scarborough, and Williams. The North Carolina General Assembly noticed that the colonists were not paying taxes. Thus, Ocracoke was annexed to the Carteret Precinct in 1770 and then to Hyde County in 1845. While the British tried to blockade the inlet during the War of 1812, they were unsuccessful. In May 1861, the Confederate army erected a small octagonal fort on nearby Beacon Island next to the Ocracoke Inlet. Fort Ocracoke was difficult for ships to get near, which made it a strong fortification. But with the approaching Union army overtaking the fort at Hatteras, Fort Ocracoke was quickly abandoned. Beacon Island itself was submerged by the 1933 hurricane.

Living through hurricanes became part of the story of Ocracoke. The 1772 tropical storm washed 40 boats ashore and caused 50 deaths, while cattle were killed and the beach was damaged in the hurricane of 1785. In June 1825, a hurricane hit North Carolina on a path from Cuba to New England, causing massive flooding and making 20 ships come ashore. The storm of 1913 was also fierce, and outsiders thought everyone on the island had been killed. The 1846 hurricane created the Hatteras Inlet.

The August storm of 1899 devastated the island. The wind blew at 120 to 140 miles per hour at its peak, and the waves were reported to be 20 to 30 feet high. Homes, boats, and businesses were destroyed. Redding Aycock Thompson Sr., whose family had a summer cottage on the island, recalled, "Storm clouds gathered in the early morning. By noon the water was up to our doorstep, and the winds were of gale force. . . . It was a very violent night. No one slept. Such a screeching and howling of winds, with live oak trees being blown down and against the house, with the timbers and framing of the house groaning as if the house would be smashed to pieces at any minute. . . . Our small two-story house was . . . a complete wreck after the storm. . . . The oldest people on Ocracoke said that the 'August Storm' was the worst one within the memory of living men." Major hurricanes hit again in 1933, 1944, and 1955, reshaping the landscape of Ocracoke.

With so many storms and shifting shoals, shipwrecks were commonplace. One of the earliest recorded deaths from a shipwreck was on December 5, 1819. The *Henry*, a sloop headed from New York to Charleston, wrecked in a hurricane just off of Ocracoke. Six people died. Captain Hand, who survived the wreckage for 24 hours, was the lone survivor; he was rescued by an Ocracoker. Before the 1880s, there was no lifesaving station on Ocracoke. In 1827, the Cape Hatteras Lightship, whose job it was to warn other ships of danger, sank off of Ocracoke. Captain Holden, his wife, and their three daughters survived. To assist with rescues, the Hatteras Inlet Station was built in 1883, and in 1904, the first lifeboat station was built in the village.

Ocracoke's first school was started for the children of the Life-Saving Service station at Hatteras Inlet. The school was located in the back of Ellen Robinson's house and was called Captain Wilson's School. With competition between the two opposing sides of Ocracoke, the Pointers and the Creekers, several schools emerged in the village. By 1917, Ocracoke built a unified school for the entire island. The Methodist church, too, was split between Northern and Southern factions, but by 1937, they had united into one congregation. Also in the 1930s, the Assembly of God church was built.

Communication was essential on Ocracoke, and the mail had always been an important part. The first post office on the Outer Banks was established on Ocracoke on August 21, 1840. William Hatton Howard, the great-grandson of the last colonial owner of Ocracoke, became the first postmaster. Mail arrived on the island three times per week, traveling from Marshallberg, North

Carolina, and going through several towns before traveling to Portsmouth and then Ocracoke. Mail boats and later the ferry service made mail travel faster and the island more accessible.

During World War II, Ocracokers felt they were on the front line of the war. Cape Hatteras was important for shipping, so the U-boats heavily patrolled Hatteras and Ocracoke. More ships were sunk off the Outer Banks than any other area. Ocracokers, who could hear explosions and see fires burning, were subject to frequent blackouts throughout the village. Life on the quiet island changed dramatically in 1942, when the Navy built a base. For most sailors, coming to Ocracoke was considered a difficult assignment. But even with its isolation, Ocracoke has always maintained a working knowledge of the outside world.

Ocracoke village was once separated by two ditches that cut the village into two sections. The harbor, referred to by locals as "the creek," was christened Silver Lake Harbor. Different stores have come and gone with time, but Ocracoke has remained true to the value of local small businesses. Banker ponies once roamed the island freely but are now under the protection of the National Park Service. Roads have only been paved since the 1940s, and street names did not appear until the 1990s. Ocracoke is a simpler time, with proud locals who have a brogue all their own.

Throughout its history, Ocracoke has remained a seafaring village, with the harbor as the working watermen's entrance ramp to the sound and the sea. Beginning in the 1800s, Ocracoke became a popular hunting and fishing destination. Local guides took tourists surf fishing or to hunting camps. While vacationers have enjoyed the island since its early settlement, Ocracoke did not become a beachgoing destination until the 20th century. With the establishment of the Cape Hatteras National Seashore, the National Park Service took over the upkeep of the beaches and the lighthouse grounds. In recent decades, Ocracoke has welcomed immigrant families, adding to the unique culture of the island. Ocracoke Island, known for its breathtaking beaches, scenic marshlands, peaceful harbor, and stunning sunsets, is a classic Americana keepsake and a beautiful place to call home.

A fishing boat enters "the ditch," or the entrance from the sound to the harbor. The harbor, which was first shallow, is referred to by locals as Cockle Creek or the creek. It was dredged in the 1930s and 1940s to make way for larger ships, with its official name changed to Silver Lake. Seen in the photograph is Kugler Cottage, built in 1850 on Windmill Point. (OPS.)

Turning left out of the ditch will lead one past Teach's Hole to Ocracoke Inlet. Portsmouth Island sits on the other side of the Ocracoke Inlet entrance. In the middle of the photograph is the *Benson H. Riggin* pilothouse. The *Benson H. Riggin*, a menhaden boat, ran aground in 1953. The pilothouse was moved across the ditch and became the Runyon children's playhouse. (OPS.)

One

FROM PIRATES TO PILOTS

People living on Down Point, the southern side of the island near the lighthouse, were called "Pointers." Those who lived on the northern side along the creek were called "Creekers." These labels remain today. Early in village history, a division grew between the Pointers and the Creekers. Pictured is the harbor with the Doxsee family home on the Down Point side (left) and the Ocracoke Lifeboat Station on the creek side (right). The ditch sits in between. (OPS.)

1775

The Ocracoke inlet was first labeled "Wokokon Inlet" on maps drawn by John White in 1584–1587 as part of Sir Walter Raleigh's expedition. This name is said to refer to a Native American tribe that lived along the Neuse River but used the island for hunting and fishing. In 1715, the Colonial Assembly of North Carolina, which realized the importance of trade from the Ocracoke Inlet to the mainland, passed an act that established pilots on Ocracoke to help larger ships maneuver through the dangerous shoals on the Outer Banks. In 1764, the Colony of North Carolina set aside 20 more acres for the pilots. Notice on the map at left that Hatteras and Ocracoke are joined, as this was prior to the 1846 hurricane, which isolated Ocracoke. (Left, Ellen Fulcher Cloud Collection, OPS; below, OPS.)

Though pilots were the first official residents of Ocracoke, Edward Teach is the most famous. Blackbeard was a pirate between 1716 and 1718. During that time, he wreaked havoc on ships from New England to the West Indies, capturing more than 50 ships and terrifying seagoers. On November 22, 1718, Blackbeard was killed in a naval battle offshore in what would be called Teach's Hole Channel just off Springer's Point. Lt. Robert Maynard, at the request of Virginia governor Spotswood, fought Blackbeard and his crew. Blackbeard received 20 sword wounds and five pistol wounds. His head was cut off, and his body was tossed overboard. Legend has it that Blackbeard's body swam around the ship seven times. His severed head was taken around Virginia and North Carolina to warn other pirates. (SANC.)

Mysteries surround the legend of Blackbeard. Some say that he was only a visitor for a short time on the island, using it as a hangout. Others say that he built a home here in a secluded area that is known today as Springer's Point. Historical records indicate that this area was actually settled in the 1600s. Blackbeard himself seemed to be drawn to it because of its easy access to the inlet and its secluded location. Some believe that the old home that once sat on Springer's Point belonged to Blackbeard himself. Today, only bricks and a cistern remain. However, many visitors still wander through Springer's Point hoping to discover Blackbeard's elusive treasure. (Both, Chester Lynn.)

On November 11, 1719, the Lords Proprietors of North Carolina gave John Lovick, the secretary of the Colony of North Carolina and a deputy of the Lords Proprietors, the island of Occacock. While Lovick never intended to live on the island, he wanted to put his livestock on the land for grazing. He was given approximately 2,110 acres. On July 30, 1759, William Howard Sr. purchased the island. He was the fourth colonial owner and the first to live on Ocracoke. Richard Sanderson Sr. and Richard Sanderson Jr. were the second and third colonial owners, and it is suggested that William Howard married into their family. It has also been a theory that Howard served as Blackbeard's quartermaster in 1718. Pictured here is the George Howard family cemetery with one of the oldest graves on the island, believed to be that of George Howard, the first son of William Howard Sr. He was born in 1749 and died in 1806. (OPS.)

Royal Governor Josiah Martin wrote in January 1778, "The contemptible Port of Ocracock . . . has become a great Channel of supply to the Rebels while the more considerable Ports of the Continent have been watched by the King's Ships." Indeed, Ocracoke Inlet was very important to the Patriots during the American Revolution. The North Carolina Provincial Congress created a company of soldiers on Ocracoke in 1776. Some familiar Ocracoke surnames were among the members: James Wahob, John Brag, and John Williams. The latter, according to Philip Howard's Blog *Ocracoke Island Journal*, may have been the same man who purchased half of Ocracoke in 1759 from William Howard. (Both, OPS.)

Between 1798 and 1810, the first lighthouse in the area was located on Shell Castle, three miles off Ocracoke Island. After the Revolutionary War, Ocracoke Inlet became even more vital to the trade industry. In 1789, North Carolina granted five islands in Ocracoke Inlet to John Gray Blount of Washington, North Carolina, and John Wallace of Portsmouth—Dry Sand Shoal, Beacon Island, Long Dry Rock, Old Rock, and Remus' Rock. Old Rock was renamed Shell Castle, where the two men built a shipping and trading center, as displayed on the pitcher. Shell Castle had warehouses, a mill, a windmill, a store, a fish house, and two homes. Wallace became governor of Shell Castle, and a pyramid-shaped lighthouse made of wood and cedar shingles was built in 1798. It stood 55 feet tall, and the light came from a four-wick whale-oil lamp. Twenty-eight people lived on Shell Castle by 1810. Today, Shell Castle is underwater. (OPS.)

Prior to the War of 1812, Ocracoke Inlet was one of the busiest waterways along the East Coast. Privateers used this route to reach the mainland. Knowing this, the British started a campaign led by Rear Adm. Sir George Cockburn against Portsmouth and Ocracoke Island. On the night of July 11, 1813, the British entered the inlet with a 74-gun man-of-war, three frigates, a brig, three schooners, and close to 3,000 British soldiers. They captured two ships, the French ship *Atlas* (filled with a cargo of silk) and the brig *Anaconda* (a private boat that was authorized by the US government to capture enemy vessels). This watercolor shows the capture of the *Anaconda*. Three hundred British troops and 400 sailors, under the command of Lt. Col. Charles Napier, landed on Ocracoke and Portsmouth Islands. The soldiers killed one civilian, Richard Carey of Portsmouth, who was trying to escape with his family. The British also killed 400 sheep, 200 cattle, and 1,600 waterfowl. (MM.)

THE WAR IN AMERICA :—FORT OCRACOKE, ON BEACON ISLAND, NORTH CAROLINA, DESTROYED BY FIRE ON THE 17TH ULT, BY THE FEDERALISTS.

During the Civil War, a Confederate fort was built on Beacon Island at the site where a fort had been during the War of 1812. Just a mile off of Ocracoke, the fort was constructed on the day that North Carolina seceded from the Union, May 20, 1861. Fort Ocracoke was sturdy, octagonal in shape, and held around 500 troops. On August 28, 1861, Fort Hatteras and Fort Clark were captured by the Union. Four companies from Fort Ocracoke and Portsmouth Island had been called to Hatteras to fight, leaving an insecure Fort Ocracoke behind. The frightened soldiers soon abandoned Fort Ocracoke. By mid-September, Union forces found Fort Ocracoke completely empty. They blew up the fort on September 17. (Both, SANC.)

THE CIVIL WAR IN AMERICA : CAMP WINFIELD, HATTERAS INLET, NORTH CAROLINA.—FROM A SKETCH BY OUR SPECIAL ARTIST.—SEE PAGE 262.

In 1855, Daniel Tolson purchased the land that was once Blackbeard's hangout, where Tolson lived with his family and 22 slaves. The censuses from 1790 to 1860 show that there were from 16 to over 100 slaves on Ocracoke during that period. According to author David S. Cecelski, in his book *The Waterman's Song: Slavery and Freedom in Maritime North Carolina*, "The African Americans at Ocracoke Inlet were mainly skilled watermen and their families." At the end of the Civil War, former slaves fled Ocracoke. One couple, Harkus Blount and Winnie Bragg Blount (pictured), both former slaves, moved to the island. Winnie and Harkus had two children. Their daughter, Jane, married Leonard Bryant, a coworker at the Doxsee Clam Factory. They had 13 children, including Muzel Bryant. Winnie lived to be 105 years old, and her granddaughter, Muzel, lived to be 103. For more than 100 years, member of the Blount family were the only African Americans to live on Ocracoke. (OPS.)

Two

KEEPERS OF THE LIGHT

The Ocracoke Lighthouse was instrumental in helping ships navigate the dangerous shoals. The light on the Ocracoke Lighthouse was first a whale-oil lamp. In 1854, this was replaced by a Fresnel lens. The Confederate troops took out the Fresnel lens in 1862, but the Union army returned it in 1863. Later, the lamp was changed to a 100-watt incandescent bulb. (SANC.)

In 1820, William Williams, John Williams, Joseph Williams, William Howard Jr., and Henry Garrish offered the federal government land on which to build the Ocracoke Island Lighthouse. Jacob Gaskill sold the government an adjacent parcel of land in 1822 for $50. The lighthouse was built on Jacob Gaskill's land by Noah Porter of Massachusetts in 1823 for $11,359.35. It stands 75 feet tall and can be seen for 14 miles offshore. Its brick walls are five feet thick at the base, and it has a spiral staircase inside. Joshua Taylor was the first collector and superintendent of the lighthouse, from 1823 to 1829. Anson Harker was the first person to be recorded as the keeper, from 1847 to 1853. The image shows Ellis Howard standing in front of the lighthouse on May 24, 1893. He was the longest-serving keeper, from 1862 to 1897, and died in office. (OBHC.)

Noah Porter also built the lightkeeper's house in 1823. It was originally one story with three rooms. In 1897, a second floor was added with three additional rooms for the keeper's assistant. Beside the lighthouse, a small blockhouse was used to store the fuel, including whale oil, porpoise oil, and kerosene. A vapor lamp replaced the oil lamp in the late 1920s. By 1904, a woodshed was constructed and 324 feet of fencing built. The stairs were replaced in the 1950s. The marks made by the original steps are visible in the photograph. The Ocracoke Island Lighthouse is the oldest lighthouse in North Carolina that remains in operation. (Both, Bill Cochran Collection, OPS.)

Initially, lighthouse maintenance was an arduous task that included the keeper and his entire family. Keepers were on duty 24 hours per day, seven days a week. Rule no. 11 in the *Instructions to Light-Keepers* manual, written in July 1881, states, "A light-house must never be wholly unattended. Where there is a keeper and one or more assistants, either the keeper or one of the assistants must be present. If there is only one keeper, some member of his family, or other responsible person, must be at the station in his absence." (Left, OBHC; below, SANC.)

At sunset, the keeper had to light the lamp, making sure it remained lit all night and extinguishing it at sunrise. Fuel had to be refilled, the wick trimmed, and the lantern room windows polished. The entrance into the lantern room was just a hatch through the floor big enough for only one person. The Fresnel lens encompassed most of the room itself, leaving little space between the lens and the windows. The door to the outside balcony was only three feet high. The buildings on the lighthouse grounds had to be maintained. A daily logbook was compiled, complete with weather information, tides, and inventories. Lighthouse keepers were even expected to take visitors on tours of the lighthouse throughout the day. (Right, OBHC; below, SANC.)

In its history, the Ocracoke Island Lighthouse has had a total of 12 keepers. The last to be employed by the US Lighthouse Service was Capt. Joe Burrus, who was the keeper for 16 years. He was born on Hatteras Island; his father had been a captain who was lost at sea when Joe was a child. Prior to serving as lighthouse keeper, Joe sailed on a freighter. He joined the US Lighthouse Service in 1903. In 1929, Joe began his service on Ocracoke with his wife and children. Upon his retirement, he built a home on the edge of the village that today is Oscar's House Bed and Breakfast. Captain Joe retired in 1946 as the last keeper to serve under the US Lighthouse Service. Clyde Farrow, a Buxton native, served as the lighthouse keeper on Ocracoke until 1954, when the lighthouse was automated and put in the care of the Coast Guard. The keeper's quarters and the grounds are maintained by the National Park Service. (OPS.)

Three

HEROES OF THE STORMS

The waters off the Outer Banks are known as the "Graveyard of the Atlantic," as dangerous shoals and rough seas have caused hundreds of shipwrecks. Lightship stations were built to help vessels navigate these waters. Ocracoke Channel Lightship Station (1852–1859) was located at the entrance to the inlet, around 300 yards from the southern end of the island. (SANC.)

Diamond Shoals, just off of Hatteras, is one of the most dangerous areas of the Atlantic to navigate. The US Life-Saving Service officially began on August 14, 1848, with the signing of the Newell Act, although volunteers and private citizens had been assisting shipwreck victims all along. Ocracoke's first lifeboat station was built in 1883. It was located at the northern end of the island (where the Hatteras ferry runs today). It was called both the Hatteras Inlet Station and the Cedar Hammock Station. Several families lived in the Cedar Hammock community, which also had its own school. Making $700 per year, Capt. James Howard became the first keeper of the station. He served in this capacity for 20 years. Capt. James Howard is seen in this early photograph with his wife, Zilphia Williams Howard. (Philip Howard.)

Since it was difficult for the crew at the Hatteras Inlet Station to reach boats in danger outside of the Ocracoke Inlet, the need for a second lifeboat station arose. This became evident two days before Christmas in 1894. The *Richard S. Spofford*, a schooner traveling from Boston to Georgia, went aground in the Ocracoke Inlet, getting pounded by the stormy sea for hours. With the help of Ocracokers, five crewmen made it to shore in a small boat, but the rest of the crew had to wait a full day for the rescuers to get from the Hatteras Inlet Station to the wreck. One crew member died. The Ocracoke Lifeboat Station was built in 1904 with David Williams as the first keeper. The Ocracoke Lifeboat Station became the Ocracoke Coast Guard Station in 1915, when the Life-Saving Service merged with the Revenue Cutter Service to form the Coast Guard. (OPS.)

In 1917, the Hatteras Inlet Station was replaced by a new Coast Guard station on the northern end of the island, or "Down Below," as locals referred to that part of the island. It operated as a Coast Guard station until 1953, when it was decommissioned due to beach erosion and the incoming surf, which made the building vulnerable. The structure itself was destroyed by Hurricane Ione, which pummeled the island for 18 hours in 1955. Today, pilings can often still be seen at the northern end near the Hatteras Inlet ferry docks. (Both, Charles Brown Collection, OPS.)

The Ocracoke Lifeboat Station that opened in 1904 was replaced with a new one just before World War II. The new Coast Guard station was built in the 1940s for $160,000. It was a vital part of the lives of the islanders. It was the only place on the island where a telegram could be sent or a phone call could be made. During World War II, a building was added to the left of the station, as seen in the image below, in which soldiers whose ships had been attacked by U-boats would wait for transportation off the island. By 1996, the Coast Guard abandoned the station, moving it to Hatteras. It later became the North Carolina Center for the Advancement of Teaching. (Both, OPS.)

Ben Gaskill was the cook at the Hatteras Inlet Coast Guard Station. In 1927, Charles Lindbergh landed on Ocracoke. Darkness and weather forced his landing as he was making his trip around the country in the *Spirit of St. Louis*. Lindbergh was lodged for the night at the Coast Guard station. When Lindbergh arrived unrecognized, everyone had finished his meal, and Gaskill was cleaning up. He was asked to prepare one more plate for a single visitor. Upon seeing the guest, Gaskill immediately recognized him and said, "Why you look like that Lindbergh fella." Lindbergh commented that evening that he had the best baked beans he had ever eaten. (OPS.)

THE WRECK OF THE STEAM BOAT HOME,
Off Ocracock, on Monday, October 9ᵗʰ 1837.
Ninety-five lives lost.

Hundreds of shipwrecks occurred between the 1800s and the 1900s, keeping Life-Saving stations on constant watch. One of Ocracoke's worst shipwrecks was that of the *Home* in 1837. She was a 220-foot steamship traveling from New York to Charleston with 130 passengers. She met a hurricane near Cape Hatteras, called the Racer's Storm, which had formed near Jamaica, crossed into the Gulf of Mexico, and then moved back across the southeastern United States to the Atlantic. The *Home* got stuck on a shoal six miles outside of Ocracoke village. Unfortunately, it was 10:00 at night, and the crew was unable to get the attention of the villagers. A lifeboat was lowered with 15 to 20 people aboard, only to have all of its passengers topple into the sea. Ninety people died, and 40 made it to safety. Most of the bodies were found the next day, strewn with the wreckage along Ocracoke's shore. The following year, Congress passed the Steamboat Act, requiring every offshore vessel to have one life jacket per person. (MM.)

On Christmas Eve, 1899, the *Ariosto* ran aground three miles from the Hatteras Inlet Station. She was traveling from Texas to Germany by way of Norfolk. Some sailors remained onboard, but 21 left in lifeboats and drowned. The *Sacramento Record Union* reported, "Captain Baines and eight of the crew were saved by the heroic efforts of the Ocracoke life-saving crew, under Captain James Howard." (MM.)

The six-masted schooner *George W. Wells* weighed 2,970 tons; she was one of the largest wooden sailing vessels ever built. On September 3, 1913, hurricane-force winds caused the ship to run aground near the present-day pony pen. All aboard were saved in a very heroic rescue made by both Life-Saving stations. Pieces of the wreck may be found on Ocracoke. (SANC.)

The *Carroll A. Deering*, better known as the "Ghost Ship," was a large five-masted schooner on a trip from Barbados to Hampton Roads, Virginia. On January 19, 1921, she passed the lightship keepers at the Cape Lookout Lightship and the Diamond Shoals Lightship. The latter reported at 5:45 p.m. that the *Deering*'s course seemed odd. The Cape Hatteras Coast Guard spotted the grounded ship on the morning of January 31. When the ship was boarded, she was found neat and clean. The table had been set. But no crew members or personal belongings were found, only a gray cat. The Coast Guard dynamited the ship. Some pieces floated onto Ocracoke's northern shore, where wind covered the remains with sand. They were exposed again after the 1955 hurricane and floated once more to Hatteras on high tide. (Both, OPS.)

Ocracokers were often beneficiaries of wrecked cargo. On August 23, 1925, the *Victoria S.* scattered lumber onshore. She ran aground about two miles outside of the Ocracoke Inlet and broke apart in the surf. The owners of the cargo were contacted, and two Ocracokers, Capt. Bill Gaskill and Albert Styron, helped with the salvage of the lumber. On December 3, 1927, the Norwegian freighter *Cibao*, pictured here, spilled 17,000 bunches of bananas on Ocracoke's shore. Luckily, the crew was rescued after being discovered by the lookout at Hatteras Inlet Station. Ocracokers had bananas for weeks, and many Ocracoke children complained of a stomachache. (MM.)

On Saturday, August 17, 1935, the three-masted schooner *Nomis*, headed to Georgetown, South Carolina, from New York, wrecked six miles off of Hatteras Inlet. Hatteras Inlet Station captain Bernice Ballance and Ocracoke Inlet Station captain Elisha Tillet responded quickly. The *Nomis*, the last large schooner to wreck on Ocracoke, carried 338,000 feet of lumber. The photograph, taken by Selma Wise Spencer, a member of the Ocracoke School faculty, shows salvage efforts underway. Walter O'Neal is seen tipping his hat. Many homes were built from lumber taken from shipwrecks. (Both, Selma Wise Spencer Collection, OPS.)

On March 1, 1942, *Anna R. Heidritter*, traveling from Charleston to Pennsylvania, wrecked near Hatteras Inlet. Members of the nine-person crew tied themselves to the masts to avoid going into the water. The *Heidritter* was one of the last 20th-century sailing ships to wreck off North Carolina. Sadly, just a little over a week after being rescued, the captain, Bennett Coleman, died in a car accident. (OPS.)

January 1, 1948, was a beautiful New Year's Day. The *Charlie Mason*, an Outer Banks pogey boat, was fishing just offshore of Ocracoke. But the weather changed, and the *Charlie Mason* found herself in trouble. She went ashore in sight of the Wahab Village Hotel. Charles Stowe, a member of the Coast Guard who was aboard the ship, wrote the ballad "The *Charlie Mason* Pogey Boat." (OPS.)

Four

JUST GETTING THERE

Footbridges connected the south side and the north side of the village. Two streams ran from Cockle Creek, beside the Island Inn, towards the marsh that led out to the beach. These streams, called "guts" by the islanders, cut the village into two distinct areas—Around Creek and Down Point. They were filled in when the harbor was dredged during World War II. (OPS.)

In 1950, Capt. Frazier Peele, a Hatteras native, established the first car ferry to run from Hatteras Inlet to Ocracoke. He initially constructed it out of a skiff with a deck across the top. The following year, he built a solid ferry with rails and a ramp that could hold four cars. Peele made three trips daily, charging $5. He rarely shut down the ferry, even traveling in stormy weather. As an avid hunter, Peele kept a gun in the cabin. During hunting season, he shot ducks and geese along the route, steering the ferry to pick up the fallen birds along the way. (Left, OPS; below, SANC.)

Once at Ocracoke, the Peele ferry was unable to get close enough to shore, so cars departed into the shallow water and drove to the beach. Charlie McWilliams's mail truck, pictured above driving through the water, was on the ferry six days a week. It would take "Charlie Mac" an hour to travel the unpaved road from Hatteras Inlet to the village. Hopefully it would be low tide to make driving through the sand a little easier. Once a vehicle was in the village, the unpaved roads were covered with sand. The "Main Road," as it was called, extended from the beach all the way to the sound at the northern end of the village. It included Howard Street, the village street that remains unpaved even today. (Above, OPS; below, OBHC.)

Charlie Caswell McWilliams was an Ocracoke legend. He was a master decoy carver and an avid cigar smoker. According to Philip Howard's blog, Charlie Mac often included a note with his decoys that read, "The wood in this hand-carved decoy came from one of the five masts of the schooner *Carroll A. Deering*, wrecked in a great storm on Diamond Shoals off Cape Hatteras more than forty years ago. . . . After she had been dynamited, one section of this famous Ghost Ship was driven ashore at Ocracoke Island in another storm, where I salvaged a mast. I carved this body from the mast, carved the head out of a natural driftwood knee found on the beach, and then painted the decoy." His grandfather, John Small McWilliams, moved to Ocracoke from Washington, North Carolina, at the start of the Civil War to be a teacher. Charlie Mac's father owned a store on Cockle Creek and became the postmaster in 1883. (WLUNC.)

Before Frazier Peele built his ferry, Charlie Mac assumed a car shuttle service started by Walter O'Neal and Van Henry O'Neal. Stanley Wahab had received a contract to transport mail from Hatteras to Ocracoke and asked the O'Neals to carry the mail in their four-wheel-drive station wagon to the Hatteras Inlet. Van Henry, pictured at far right with his hand on his hip, drove the bus. Van Henry picked up people at home or at the Wahab Village hotel, took them to the Hatteras Inlet Coast Guard Station, and then put them on the *Armeda* to Hatteras Village. From there, passengers went with Anderson or Stockton Midgett or the Midgetts' father to Manteo, where they took a bus to Norfolk. Also pictured are Robert W. Spencer holding the suitcase and Doss Forbes. (Both, OPS.)

In 1957, the State of North Carolina bought the four-car ferry that ran between Ocracoke and Hatteras from Frazier Peele, acknowledging that Peele's entrepreneurial spirit had proven there was a need for a larger ferry system. The new state ferry was a free service to encourage the growth of the tourism industry on the island. In the early 1960s, the state purchased the vessel *Sea Level*, which provided ferry service to Cedar Island. Later, the Swan Quarter ferry was added. Both the Cedar Island and Swan Quarter ferries charge a fee. (Both, OBHC.)

Before ferries and roads, the mail was delivered on Ocracoke by boats. The first mail boat service had two boats. One would leave Morehead and the other would leave Ocracoke on the same day. It took two days for the mail to return. By the 1900s, several boats were used to transport mail, including the *Kitty Watts* and the *Ripple*. By 1928, only one mail boat traveled from Atlantic to Ocracoke. The mail boat left Atlantic daily at 1:00 p.m. Two years later, the *Aleta* took over mail boat duties. In 1931, Capt. William Goodwin Willis built a general store at the end of his dock, and this is where the mail boat would come. There, anxious Ocracokers would greet friends and family who had traveled to the island. The mail would go to the post office and get sorted. The villagers would meet at the post office, where the postmaster would step outside to "call the mail over." Names were shouted and letters were handed out. (SANC.)

Mail was also carried between Hatteras and Ocracoke by skiff. On October 21, 1902, Thomas Wallace Howard became postmaster, and he held the position for 41 years. "Mr. Tommy" took a skiff three miles once a week to get mail and passengers from Avon. In 1917, Pamlico Sound froze, trapping the mail on Portsmouth Island. Mr. Tommy, determined to get the mail and to keep Ocracokers happy, walked across the ice to retrieve the mail from Portsmouth. He erected an official building for the post office near his home on Cockle Creek. On October 12, 1937, he sent the first airmail from Ocracoke to Kitty Hawk, North Carolina. The image shows Charlie Mac loading mail onto a plane in the 1950s. When Mr. Tommy retired in 1941, his future daughter-in-law, Elizabeth O'Neal, became postmaster. (OPS.)

The *Aleta* was Ocracoke's beloved mail boat from 1930 to 1952. She was a 42-foot ship built in 1923. Her original owner was a mail carrier named Howard Nelson, who named the ship after his sister. In 1945, Elmo Fulcher and George O'Neal bought the *Aleta* and continued mail service. O'Neal sits atop the *Aleta* in this photograph. (Chester Lynn.)

Travelers were eager to get a seat on the *Aleta*. She carried up to 35 passengers during the busy summer months. The fare was $2 per person. People sat on two wooden benches under a canopy or on fish boxes and luggage on the upper deck and stern. There was a cabin where passengers could seek shelter in bad weather. (OPS.)

The *Aleta* was powered by a Caterpillar D4400 diesel engine. The engine room was on the same deck as the passenger cabin and could be quite noisy. Capt. George O'Neal, pictured, would close the door to the engine room so that passengers would not hear the roar of the engine. Captains Elmo Fulcher and O'Neal took turns spending hours a day, four days a week, in this cabin with a loud motor and small windows from which to navigate. Rotating weekly, Captains Fulcher and O'Neal would leave Ocracoke at 6:30 a.m. and arrive in Atlantic at 10:30 a.m. They would meet the mail truck and a passenger bus. After loading, the *Aleta* would leave Atlantic at 1:00 p.m. and return to Ocracoke by 5:00 p.m. Two stops were made—one in Cedar Island and the other in Portsmouth, where Henry Pigott, a resident of Portsmouth, poled a skiff to meet the *Aleta*. During World War II, the *Aleta* delivered mail, freight, and passengers for the regular citizens as well as the military. (Chester Lynn.)

Elmo and George (pictured) lost the mail contract in 1952. Elmo turned the *Aleta* into a commercial shrimp boat, and she remained that way until his death in 1979. Ansley O'Neal took over as mail boat captain on his ship the *Dolphin*. Below, the *Dolphin* enters the Ocracoke harbor. Behind the mail boat is Charlie and James Williams's fish house. The *Dolphin* was Ocracoke's last mail boat. Captain O'Neal received the last mail contract in 1952 to take mail from Atlantic to Ocracoke. He would leave Atlantic at noon and reach Ocracoke by 3:30 p.m. The *Dolphin* operated as a mail boat until 1964, when the service ended on the island. (Both, Chester Lynn.)

Elizabeth O'Neal, pictured at left, served as postmaster from 1941 to 1973. She was the daughter of Ike O'Neal and daughter-in-law of former postmaster Thomas Howard. Elizabeth had worked in her father's store as well as for Stanley Wahab as his bookkeeper. She married Wahab Howard. Upon becoming postmaster, she moved the post office to her father's store, known as Big Ike's Store or the Old Store, as seen below. This building had also served as the post office when Abner Bennett Howard had been postmaster. Big Ike's Store was damaged in the 1944 hurricane. It stood where Captain's Landing is today. (Left, OPS; below, OBHC.)

Postmaster Elizabeth Howard and her husband, Wahab Howard, built a small 432-square-foot building that had 150 mailboxes. The building sat close to the harbor, where the Down Point Decoy shop is today. It was moved next to the harbor and eventually became a gift shop and a candy store. In 1966, a new post office building that was 1,100 square feet was built on the site where Elizabeth had built her smaller post office. This new building had a lobby, bathrooms, a loading dock, and 464 mailboxes. There remained, as is still the case today, no home delivery of mail. Both the new building and Elizabeth Howard's building are part of Captain's Landing hotel, owned by Elizabeth's daughter Betty Helen and her husband, George. (Both, OPS.)

Pilot Bill Cochran, a retired Air Force colonel, and his wife, Ruth, lived in Buxton. Ruth loved to come to Ocracoke to find unique shells. Bill started a small flight service from Buxton to Ocracoke. Later, Bill and Ruth moved to Ocracoke and operated Silver Lake Inn, now known as the Island Inn. Their charter service flew passengers from Hatteras to Ocracoke, landing directly on the hard, sand-packed beach. The Cochrans were among many who used the beaches east of the village as a landing site. During inclement weather, Bill also carried mail. Ruth opened her own gift shop on the island. Today, her shells are on display at the Ocracoke Preservation Society. (Both, OPS.)

Until the 1960s, freight boats were Ocracoke's lifeline to the mainland and to needed goods. In the 1800s, sixty-foot-long bugeyes, which were two-masted, flat-bottom sailboats, carried supplies, merchandise, pony carts, and most importantly, ice. These bugeyes were soon powered with diesel engines and continued to be used to carry freight. Sometimes, even the deceased were put on the freight boats, with flags being flown at half-mast. The *Annie* was one of the first freight boats, and the *Bessie Virginia* was the last. The *Bessie Virginia* was 65 feet long and could carry 90 tons. Van Henry O'Neal (pictured) was her captain. She stopped working as a freight boat in the 1960s, when the Oregon Inlet Bridge was built and ferry services improved. (Both, OPS.)

Highway 12, the only road leading from Hatteras Inlet to the village of Ocracoke, was not paved until 1957. The first road consisted of three miles of steel matting and 11 miles of blacktop. With an official state highway, life in the village changed, and state regulations had to be followed. The first roads were narrow. The first car accident occurred on Ocracoke in 1925. Capt. Bill Gaskill and Albert Styron were assisting the owners of the cargo that was aboard the shipwrecked *Victoria S.* by salvaging lumber from the shore. The cars were going in opposite directions when they both sped up into a curve and crashed head-on. Theirs were the only two cars on the island at the time. (Above, OPS; below, Ellen Fulcher Cloud Collection, OPS.)

Five

A WAY OF LIFE

Hunting camps were built Down Below, a remote area on the sound side of the island between the village and Hatteras Inlet. Quawk Hammock Camp and Green Island Club were two of the bigger camps. There were smaller, personal hunting camps as well. Pictured in 1933 are Cass Williams (left) and Charlie Williams. They built the Molasses Creek Fish and Hunting Camp. (OPS.)

The Green Island Club was first owned by a group of friends from Pittsburgh, Pennsylvania, in 1923. It was built on land purchased from Franklin and George O'Neal. Sam Jones later acquired the property to entertain hunters and fishermen. Stanley Wahab bought the Quawk Hammock Hunting Club (pictured) from its original owner, a District of Columbia art critic. Capt. Bill Gaskill owned a hunting club on Beacon Island. (OPS.)

Before the Migratory Bird Treaty Act of 1918, hunters on Ocracoke shot and sold many birds per day. They packed the birds with feathers in flour barrels, often with a stovepipe filled with ice placed in the middle. They shipped the birds to New York by way of Norfolk or Morehead City, New Bern, or Washington, North Carolina. Market hunting was how many Ocracokers made their livelihoods. (OPS.)

In the winter months, islanders and visitors hunted. At the turn of the century, flocks of geese, brant, swans, and a variety of ducks were prolific. Market gunning was outlawed in 1918, which meant that there were strict regulations on hunting certain types of waterfowl. This made goose hunting popular on Ocracoke. (OPS.)

In 1929, eelgrass disappeared from the coast of North Carolina, and waterfowl starved. This shortened the hunting season to 30 days. The eelgrass returned in late 1930s, and so did a longer hunting season, opening in mid-November. Hunters were able to bag five geese, three redheads, and three canvasbacks; the hunting of brant remained banned. Pictured here are, from left to right, Ben Garrish, an unidentified hunter, and James Williams. (OPS.)

Shooting over live decoys was outlawed in 1935, so hunters made their own decoys. Capt. Gary Bragg was among the best decoy carvers. Captain Bragg, owner of the Cedar Grove Inn, was a market hunter turned hunting guide. He used juniper or cypress wood to carve his decoys. To do so, he used a handsaw, a hatchet, a drawing knife, and a pocket knife. (OPS.)

Before 1935, most hunters hunted from a sinkbox, a narrow watertight box with a small and narrow neck about two feet wide. Weights or iron decoys were used to hold it in place. A curtain blind was created out of concrete blocks and cement. Some hunters also used a stake blind, a box on stilts that can accommodate two hunters. (OPS.)

Born on Ocracoke in 1901, Capt. "Tony" Thurston Gaskill is known as perhaps the most knowledgeable and skilled island hunting guide and served in that capacity for 72 years. Gaskill and his wife, Helen, lived in their 1925 home that was originally built on a large area of land. Today, the home sits along Irvin Garrish Highway at the beginning of the village. His boat was the *Helen II*. According to *The Pearl of the Outer Banks*, Gaskill said that he first saw a rod and reel used on the island in 1915, when he was just 13 years old. Pictured at right is Jurd Williams. (Both, OPS.)

John White's paintings of the Outer Banks in 1585 show Native Americans using weirs. The pound nets used on Ocracoke are reminiscent of this tradition. Pound nets have three parts: a lead line, the heart, and the pound. The lead line guides fish to swim to the narrowing tunnel. Fish that do not get trapped in the tunnel swim around in the heart and return back out of the lead. When it is time to bring in the catch, boats approach the pound net, untying the top of the net and pulling slowly. This is called bunting the net. The fish are either brought in by hand or dipped out of the net. The catch is culled to keep only the legal fish; all others are put back into the water. (Both, OPS.)

In the fall, mullet migrate south just off of the beach when a cold front and a northeast wind combine. For generations, Ocracokers have haul-seined for mullet beginning sometime in mid-October. Using a similar method as the Native Americans, nets are pulled in dory boats, a flat-bottomed boat with high sides, and taken out into the water. Nets can be set and remain for many days, which requires several people to haul in the catch. A dory can also be put in the ocean while one end of the net remains connected to a truck or tractor. Fishermen take the dory into the water about 800 yards and then circle back. Today, rather than using the heavy haul-seine nets, commercial fishermen use gill nets, which require less maintenance. (Above, OBHC; below, Chester Lynn.)

For generations, Ocracokers have lived off the sea. But before 1938, commercial fishing would have been too costly and required too much time to take fish to the mainland, since there was no refrigeration. Thus, most fishermen sold their catches to one of the fish houses. With gasoline power replacing sails, commercial fishing became profitable in the 1930s and 1940s. Ten years after World War II, shrimping flourished. Some islanders would progue for a living, using a rake, gig, or tongs for flounder, clams, oysters, and even turtles. Today, Ocracoke's Working Watermen's Association supports a growing number of commercial fishermen by maintaining a fish house on Ocracoke. (Both, OPS.)

Sportfishing became popular on Ocracoke in the late 1800s, and many Ocracokers benefitted financially. In the 1940s and 1950s, Jake Alligood offered a taxicab service. Jake, seen wearing a white apron, would pick up fishermen at a hotel and drive them to the beach. He would leave them there with tackle and water and returned at a designated time. (OPS.)

Tourists also flocked to charter fishing. Ocracoke guides answered the call. Many islanders owned and operated charter boats, or party boats, to take visitors out to the sound to fish. The most sought-after fish was the red drum that arrived in mid-March. Pictured here are guides and sportsmen in front of the *Berkley*. They are, from left to right, Richard O'Neal, Owen Gaskill, five unidentified visiting sportsmen, Stevie O'Neal, Roy Parsons, and David O'Neal. Charter fishing became a vital industry in the 1950s. (OPS.)

Red drum, also known as channel bass, is the prized fish on Ocracoke. Ocracoke has a famous drum recipe sometimes called Old Drum. According to Jack Dudley's book *Ocracoke Album*, the recipe goes as follows: "Boil the drum (channel bass) until tender. Boil potatoes (with or without their jackets) separately from the drum, until done. When ready to serve, sprinkle fish with fried-out fatback cubes. Put potatoes, hard-boiled eggs, and sliced raw onions around the fish in the platter. Serve with homemade cornbread." Other popular fish found in the waters of Ocracoke include trout, mackerel, blue, cobia, and sheepshead. (Above, OBHC; below, OPS.)

Six

STAY AWHILE

For approximately two years in the late 1940s, the *Lindsey C. Warren* brought passengers from Washington, North Carolina, to Ocracoke. The ship left Washington at midnight and arrived at Ocracoke in the morning. The *Lindsey C. Warren* was an old Coast Guard 83-footer converted into a commercial vessel. Steamship service began in the late 1800s, when the Old Dominion Steamship Company transported passengers to the Ponder Hotel. (OPS.)

The Ponder Hotel was built at the site of today's decommissioned Coast Guard station in 1885 by a businessman from Washington, North Carolina. Steamboats would carry vacationers to Ocracoke for around $2 to $3. Moses Fowler served as innkeeper. The first year was so successful that eight rooms and a larger dining room were added. Between 1889 and 1899, the Spencer brothers ran the hotel, charging $10 per day or $30 per month. Their newspaper advertisement promised "Health, Strength, and Pleasure" with fishing, dancing, surf-bathing, and a plethora of fish, clams, and oysters. In 1899, George Credle of Hyde County and his brother, Griff, purchased the hotel. On Thursday, August 17, 1899, during the August storm, 25 guests waited out the hurricane in the dining room. The roof of the upstairs porch was torn off, and the dock was destroyed. The following spring, the hotel caught fire when George Credle and his boat captain tried to cook a goose on the Wilson stove. (MM.)

Capt. Bill Gaskill (1869–1935) and his wife, Annie (1879–1941), bought the Pamlico Inn in 1915. Situated at the end of Lighthouse Road, the inn was a well-loved destination for hunters, fishermen, and families. In the 1930s, three cooked meals and a room cost $11.50 per week. "Miss Annie" ran the kitchen, which was known for its delicious seafood dishes. Locals and visitors alike enjoyed the pavilion at the end of the dock that was used as a dance hall. Remembering her visits to Ocracoke and Captain Bill's family, Frances Midyette states in *Our State* magazine in 1971 that "four of the Gaskill children added spice to the summers at Pamlico Inn during the 1930's. Attractive Nell, a college student, helped as a volunteer hostess. Handsome Dave was his father's assistant. . . . Young Jim (Baum) was a constant threat with his little-boy pranks. . . . Thurston was the dean of the Ocracoke fishing guides in those young years." Captain Bill died at sea in 1935 and his son Dave took over. The Pamlico Inn was destroyed by the 1944 hurricane. (OPS.)

Around 1828, Elisha Chase and his wife, Thurza Howard, built a two-story home on three acres on Pamlico Sound. In 1834, Elisha sold the property to Thurza's brothers and took his family west. In 1868, the home was sold to Capt. Samuel Dudley Bragg, who lived there with his wife, Mariah Styron, and their seven children. Captain Bragg sold the property to his wife and children just before getting lost at sea during a storm. The Braggs' son Gary, who became the sole proprietor, turned the property into a lodge for hunters and fishermen, naming it Cedar Grove Inn. Warwick T. Boos and his wife, Margueritte, purchased the property in 1951, renamed it Sound Front Inn, and ran it until the 1970s. The inn is now owned by a former Ocracoke schoolteacher, David Senseney, and is a vacation rental. (Margueritte Boos Collection, OPS.)

The middle section of the Island Inn was built in 1901, with the Odd Fellows lodge operating upstairs and the island school downstairs. In 1920, the building became a private home to Benjamin O'Neal and was moved to its current location on Lighthouse Road. In 1940, Stanley Wahab turned it into a coffee shop, and the upstairs served as an officers' club. (OBHC.)

After the war, Robert Stanley Wahab turned what is today's Island Inn into one of Ocracoke's first modern hotels, calling it the Silver Lake Inn. First, he added a west wing that was built using barracks from the naval base. This became a dance hall that featured Saturday night square dances. (OPS.)

In the 1950s, Robert Stanley Wahab added an east wing that featured a dining room and guest rooms. The Silver Lake Inn had indoor plumbing, electricity, and a modern kitchen. A double room cost $4 per night and $21.50 per week. Years later, Doward Brugh purchased the hotel and changed the name to Island Inn. Today, the Island Inn is a historic landmark. (OPS.)

Robert Stanley Wahab was instrumental to Ocracoke's economic development. Born on February 3, 1888, to James Hatton Wahab and Martha Ann Howard, Stanley left Ocracoke at 16 but returned later to teach school. In 1914, he built the first movie theater, the Ocean Wave, and introduced the first car to Ocracoke, a Hudson coach. (OPS.)

Stanley Wahab brought electricity to Ocracoke with the building of the generator plant in 1938. With it came the luxury of refrigeration, which the islanders had not had. The Ocracoke Power and Light Company constructed a wood and concrete structure near the Community Store that housed two 60-kilowatt Worthington generators. Today, the building is home to Kitty Hawk Kites. (OPS.)

For many years, ice was transported to Ocracoke in large blocks on mail or freight boats. Those blocks were cut into pieces that would fit into iceboxes for homes. When electricity was introduced to the island, an ice plant was built next to the electric plant. This image shows the power and light company with the Northern Methodist Church in the background. (OPS.)

Stanley Wahab began a flying service from Manteo to Ocracoke, started a mail route from Hatteras, financed the first ferry, and helped get Cockle Creek dredged and roads paved. In 1935, he opened the Spanish Casino Dance Hall with its adobe facade, flat roof, and decorative windows. An open porch faced the beach, and the inside featured a dance floor surrounded by benches. (OPS.)

Built in 1938, Stanley Wahab's most extensive project was the Wahab Village Hotel, later renamed Blackbeard's Lodge. Along with offering hotel rooms that had private baths, Wahab Village Hotel became the island's entertainment center for visitors and locals. One wing held a roller-skating rink, and the other held a movie theater. (OPS.)

The front of the Wahab Village Hotel is pictured with the Spanish Casino on the right. In the middle is the old laundry facility run by Iva Spencer O'Neal. The Wahab Village Hotel was the first to have electric power and a telephone switchboard. Today, the hotel is called Blackbeard's Lodge. It is run by Stanley Wahab's great-grandnephew Stanley "Chip" Stevens and his wife, Helena. (OPS.)

Clyde Willis, pictured here, was the first innkeeper of the Wahab Village Hotel. He was followed by Clenon Boyette, who first visited Ocracoke in 1941 after he applied for a job with Hyde County Schools. Clenon became principal of Ocracoke School in the fall of 1941. He and his wife, Beulah, took over the hotel soon after and managed it until 1965. (OPS.)

The hotel sat on the edge of what Ocracokers called "the Plains," a flat, sandy stretch of land that had little vegetation. Often, the tide would come close to the front of the hotel. Aircraft would land on the Plains and bring visitors very close to the hotel doors. When Highway 12 was paved and the dunes were built by the National Park Service, the area filled with bushes, shrubs, and trees. Soon, houses and businesses were built. Beyond and to the left of the lighthouse in this image is Silver Lake Inn, and just beyond that stands the Wahab Village Hotel, with the Plains stretching all the way to the ocean. (OPS.)

Seven

O'COCKERS AND GATHERING PLACES

Ocracoke Island had four windmills; the location of each remains unclear. Oral histories indicate that Job Wahab had a windmill on his property on the harbor near the ditch. Today, this area of Ocracoke is called Windmill Point. Ocracokers would exchange fish for corn on the mainland to be milled. The windmill would have looked similar to the one pictured. (SANC.)

J.H. Doxsee, originally from Long Island, built the Doxsee House and Clam Factory next to the ditch on Windmill Point. At the factory, clams were processed as clam juice, whole clams, and clam chowder. The first Doxsee Clam Factory was located in Islip, New York, where James Harvey Doxsee grew up. In the late 1800s, clams were limited in New York. James Harvey's son Henry moved the main factory to Ocracoke in 1897, bringing his wife, Carrie, and their five children. Local fishermen harvested the clams, which were then steamed in the factory. The steamed clams were moved onto wooden tables, where island women would pick through them. The clams were then put in boxes, washed, and packed. The Doxsees' two-story house sat on the harbor, facing Cockle Creek. They also built a hunting lodge and a boardinghouse where they held dances. By 1910, the factory shut down, because the clams had been overharvested. The factory moved to Florida, and Ocracokers Charlie and Sue Scarborough and their nephew Thad Gaskins followed. (Chester Lynn.)

Harvey Doxsee's son James Harvey Doxsee and his wife, Lottie, bought property on the north side of Cockle Creek. At least five of their 10 children were born on Ocracoke. Henry Birdsall Doxsee was their fourth child and died at the age of two. He is buried at the Community Cemetery on Ocracoke. Two of their children would continue to live in North Carolina. One was Helen Doxsee, who married Ambrose Burgess, pastor of the Ocracoke Methodist Episcopal Church. It is difficult to imagine such a large factory on Windmill Point. The buildings were abandoned, and by the 1930s, the house was gone and other structures were in disrepair. No sign of the factory remains today. (Above, OBHC; below, SANC.)

Ocracoke native Isaac Willis O'Neal was born on July 30, 1865, to Willis Williams O'Neal and Elizabeth Scarborough O'Neal. He married Martha Helen Williams, daughter of James Horatio Williams and Martha O'Neal. Big Ike first went to sea at 14 and throughout his life sailed on 21 different schooners, four of which were built on Ocracoke. He worked for the US Life-Saving Service at the Hatteras Inlet Station, Ocracoke Inlet Station, and Portsmouth Island. He owned a general store, initially across from his home on Howard Street. Then he purchased the store owned by A.B. Howard on Cockle Creek. Stanley Wahab operated a furniture store out of the land side of the building, and Big Ike's daughter, Elizabeth, ran the post office from the harbor side. The store was destroyed in the 1944 hurricane. (Both, OPS.)

In 1880, John Wilson McWilliams built a late-Victorian-style home on a large lot close to Cockle Creek. Cattle and sheep roamed the lawn. In the 1920s, a department store, fish house, and net house were located in front of the home on the harbor, pictured above. The dock to the far right is also seen below. The department store sold furniture and other household goods but went out of business during the Depression. When McWilliams contracted tuberculosis, Amasa Fulcher managed the store. The 1944 hurricane demolished the buildings on the harbor, but the house remained. McWilliams left, giving the house to Charlie Mac and his wife, Hilda Tolson McWilliams. Keith and Isabel McDermott bought the property and restored it in 1986. The below image also features the lighthouse dock. (Both, OPS.)

Amasa Fulcher opened the Community Store in 1918. "Mace," as he was called, left the McWilliams department store to open a store on the creek side that would soon become a hub of community activity. The store's main entrance faced Cockle Creek, or Silver Lake. Porch benches were a gathering place. The store had a potbellied stove and sold clothes, fabric, food, dishes, oil, gas, and chicken and horse feed. Coffins were also sold—they always kept two adult-size in stock and one child's. Texaco Oil was sold at the dock. Mace died in 1946, and the store was sold to Isaac Freeman O'Neal, known as "Little Ike," and his son-in-law Jesse Garrish. (Both, OPS.)

The store kept its official name as the Community Store, but locals called it Garrish and O'Neal's. The two men built a larger store, of which Jesse Garrish became the sole proprietor. The business thrived. During the hot summer months, teenagers and adults would gather on the porch to talk and eat Mayola ice cream. Whittlers would also create their masterpieces, often making birds whose wings were constructed out of the leftover wooden ice-cream spoons. The store was in business for 80 uninterrupted years and has since been revived as one of the island's beloved gathering places, owned by Joseph and Lauren Ramunni. This image, taken around 1942, shows Big Ike's Store on the harbor to the right. The next building down with the hip roof is the Community Store. Below that is the power and light company. The last building on the lower left is an appliance shop, which was later turned into a dance hall. (OPS.)

The area today affectionately called Springer's Point was named after the family who purchased the land in 1883. E.D. and Clara Springer were from South Creek, North Carolina. They did not live on Ocracoke permanently, nor were they the first owners of the property. The photograph shows the children enjoying the beautiful live oaks and cedars that flourish on the point. (Chester Lynn.)

When John Williams purchased half of Ocracoke from William Howard Sr., the area now known as Springer's Point was included. The land changed owners numerous times over the next 100 years, being referred to both as Williams' Point and Howard's Point. The house itself was two houses put together, built before 1800. Legend has it that this could have been the dwelling of Blackbeard. (OPS.)

Daniel Tolson bought the property from William Hatton Howard in 1855. Daniel added a tower to the house that rose above the trees from which he could see the Atlantic Ocean and Pamlico Sound, easily spotting any ship that approached. He is buried on the property. The Springers were next to acquire the land and then sold it to Sam Jones. (Chester Lynn.)

Sam Jones purchased 50 acres at Springer's Point in 1941. As the earliest settlement site on Ocracoke, the point had several structures, including a house, a stable, a shed or jail, and a round brick well. The area was never developed, and all the buildings were destroyed. Jones and his horse, Ikey D, are buried there. Today, it is a nature preserve. (Chester Lynn.)

Sam Jones, born in Hyde County in 1893, worked for the Berkley Iron Works and Foundry Company in Norfolk, Virginia, in his early 20s. Six years later, he purchased the company. As a child, Sam visited Ocracoke during the Fourth of July and participated in the pony pennings. In 1939, he returned to the island with his first wife, Mary Ruth Kelly, an Ocracoke native. She was the daughter of Neva May Howard and granddaughter of Capt. George Gregory Howard. By the 1950s, Sam was investing in the island, hiring locals for jobs including guides, cooks, and housekeepers. He owned the Green Island Hunt Club and built Berkley Manor, Berkley Castle, the Whittlers' Club, and the Homeplace, his family home. (Both, OBHC.)

In the 1950s, Sam Jones built Berkley Manor on land purchased from Luther and Dezzie Fulcher. It boasts 20 rooms, numerous fireplaces, and a tower. Berkley Castle, Sam's second home, was the largest structure on Ocracoke. Completed in 1955, it had 16 rooms and 32 dormer windows. For both homes, Sam used only local workers and, according to legend, did not use blueprints or plans. (OBHC.)

Berkley Castle would become Jones's guesthouse, and Berkley Manor was used for storage. Sam Jones constructed the Homeplace as his family's dwelling. Today, Berkley Manor is owned by the Simmons family and is used as a vacation rental. Berkley Castle, on Silver Lake, is a popular bed-and-breakfast. The Homeplace remains a private residence of the Jones family. (OPS.)

Sam Jones built the Whittlers' Club for carvers. Members had to follow a few rules: no one was allowed to get drunk except Harry O'Neal; the only way a member could lose membership was by telling smutty jokes; all true-story instances were always invited; and the preachers of the Methodist church and the Church of God would pass on all cases of misconduct. (WLUNC.)

Jones, whose second wife was a weaver, placed four looms inside his house. In her book *A Blessed Life: Growing up on Ocracoke Island*, native Della Gaskill recalls, "It were me, Miss Wilma, Miss Ruby, Miss Boos, Louise, Fannie Jones, Mrs. Doris, Annie Moore, and Sue D. Fleig . . . we made material and rugs and bags and all kinds of things for the Castle and Manor." (OBHC.)

In the center of the above view of Berkley Castle from the lighthouse is a home currently owned by the Gallahers. They moved the structure in 2014 from its location on Creek Road. The original house was built at the beginning of the 20th century, and an addition was built in the 1920s. The two buildings in the front right corner are Clarence Scarborough's store and home. According to Della Gaskill, Scarborough's grocery store was a place for teenagers to gather in the evenings, because it had a jukebox and a pool table. It was later purchased by Corky and Maxine Mason and is still known today as Corky's Store. (Both, OPS.)

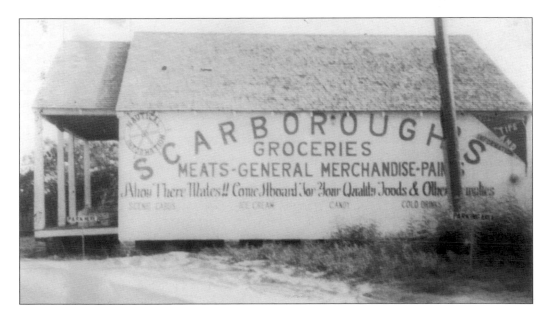

Albert Styron's Store was owned by Albert and his wife, Mamie. In 1920, Albert floated wood from Hog Island to Ocracoke to build the structure. The family home sat behind and had the distinction of having one of the first television sets on the island. In March 1956, Albert left to seed oyster beds and never returned. The search for Albert lasted 120 hours and included the mounted Boy Scouts. His 18-foot boat was recovered with his wallet, Social Security card, and watch. His son, Albert Jr., took over the store. As a grocery, it had dry goods, meat, and vegetables. It was also a great spot for candy and ice cream. Albert Jr. is said to have "mommicked" his younger patrons in those days, which is Ocracoke brogue meaning teased or bothered. Snowstorms are rare on Ocracoke, but they do occur. The image shows Albert Styron's store, which became a great gathering place for locals but closed upon Albert Jr.'s death in 1975. The March snowstorm in 1980 dumped two feet of snow on the island. (OPS.)

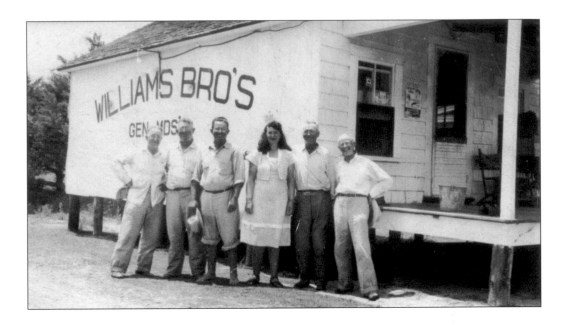

James Williams and Charlie Williams opened a small store on Lighthouse Road called Williams Bros. where they sold meats, drinks, canned goods, hot dogs, hamburgers, milkshakes, and snowballs. In Carl Goerch's 1956 book, *Ocracoke*, the author claims that the palm tree in front of the Williams Bros. store was the largest, northernmost palm tree on the Atlantic Coast. The tree stood in Floyd Styron's front yard. It had been planted by a Styron, who had gotten it as prize for selling a weekly publication. It was just a small shoot when it arrived but thrived where it was planted. The building in which the Williams Bros. store was located had been used as living quarters by the Navy. On the far left, the steeple of the original Assembly of God church is visible. (Both, Chester Lynn.)

Jake and Myra Alligood owned the Channel Bass Inn, known as "Old Jake's Place," on Back Road. Ocracoke kids loved to hang out and dance to the jukebox. Jake is pictured in the center of this photograph taken in 1955, along with his friends, from left to right, Mr. Hoffman (Raleigh), Mr. Warren (Washington, DC), Dr. Wiggins (Winston-Salem), and Mr. Getty (Knoxville). Inside the store, Jake sold ice cream, soft drinks, and cigarettes. The walls were lined with wooden benches, and the middle served as a dance floor. (OPS.)

Looking up the sandy lane that is British Cemetery Road, the house on the left belonged to Robert Benjamin O'Neal and Fanny Williams O'Neal. Charles Minor O'Neal owned the store on the right, operated by Christopher Farrow Gaskill. The home on the right belonged to Howard Kelly O'Neal and Martha Lorena Garrish O'Neal and today is Cathy Scarborough's Over the Moon gift shop. (OPS.)

This bungalow was built in 1936 using some of the wood from the schooner *Nomis*. An outbuilding, once the kitchen of the old Life-Saving station, held the bodies of the British soldiers who washed ashore. Robert Wahab and Elizabeth O'Neal Howard bought the house in 1942. Robert, who was stationed at the Navy base, ran the first electric plant. Elizabeth was the beloved postmistress. (OPS.)

Capt. David Williams, first keeper of the Ocracoke Lifeboat Station, and his wife, Alice Wahab Williams, purchased land from William H. Wahab in 1890 for $10. The home they built features five rooms upstairs and four downstairs. It was moved in 1989 from its original site near present-day Anchorage Inn to National Park Service property. Today, it houses the Ocracoke Preservation Museum. (OPS.)

Walter O'Neal's store sat where Silver Lake Motel is today. O'Neal would churn his own ice cream, running a flag up a flagpole to signal it was ready. Pictured on the store's porch are, from left to right, Russell Henley, Sam Jones, Homer Howard, Walter O'Neal Sr., William Jones, Howard C. Jones, (possibly) Mildred Bryant, Charles Jones, and Mary Ruth Jones. The store was destroyed in the 1944 hurricane. (OPS.)

Will Willis built a store and fish house on Cockle Creek. By the late 1950s, the mail boat moored at Willis's dock, where people would gather in anticipation of its arrival. When Will's son Jack took over, several charter fishing boats docked there. In the 1970s, Jack added a pool table and pinball machines. The building is now home to the Ocracoke Working Watermen's Association exhibit. (Chester Lynn.)

Capt. William Charles Thomas was born on March 23, 1857. He married Ocracoke native Eliza Gaskill in 1890 and served as first mate on the steamer *Ocracoke*. Captain Thomas received land along Cockle Creek to build on. He asked his brother-in-law, Charlie Scarborough, to build a home reminiscent of what he had seen in St. Kitts. The home was L-shaped with a double front porch facing the creek. Charlie also incorporated a trapdoor in the living room that would allow floodwaters to come through so that the house would not wash off its foundation. Captain Thomas and Eliza had gardens, a smokehouse, and a general store not too far from their home. Pictured below is Eliza Thomas on the porch of her home with her mother, Ocracoke schoolteacher Sarah Owens. (Both, OPS.)

Sarah Ellen O'Neal Gaskill was born on November 9, 1879, on Ocracoke to Howard and Charlotte O'Neal. Her father and her husband, Benjamin Gaskill, were both fishermen. As a young lady, Sarah Ellen worked at the Doxsee Clam Factory. She and Benjamin had five sons and were married for 46 years. Sarah Ellen died on September 22, 1984, close to her 105th birthday. Her mother, Charlotte Ann O'Neal (pictured below), lived to be 96. "Aunt Lott," as she was known, became one of the island's famous midwives. From 1861 to 1898, Esther Gaskins O'Neal, known as "Aunt Hettie Tom," was the island midwife, delivering around 550 babies and keeping precise records of her deliveries. She was a second cousin by marriage to Aunt Lott. In *Ocracokers*, Alton Ballance quotes Sarah Ellen: "My mother tried to keep count of all the babies she had delivered. She lost count around 100." (Left, OPS; below, Vince O'Neal.)

Kathleen Bragg was the first Ocracoker to become a registered nurse and return back to the island to practice. She was born and raised in a home near the lighthouse, as shown at right. Her grandfather Samuel Dudley Bragg was a pilot in Ocracoke's early days, as was her father, Hallis A. Bragg. Kathleen went to nursing school in Rocky Mount, North Carolina, in 1923. She became a nurse on the island in the late 1920s, and in 1953, she became employed by the Hyde County Health Department as a school nurse, where Wednesdays were called "shot days." She is seen below leaving the school. Kathleen delivered over 100 babies on Ocracoke. She died in 1975. (Both, OPS.)

Theodore Rondthaler and his wife, Alice, visited Ocracoke in the 1930s, traveling aboard the *Aleta* with Alice's ailing mother. Two hours in, with no land in sight, Alice's mother spoke her first words in several years: "Where in the hell are you taking me?" Theodore was born in Old Salem on August 5, 1899. Alice was born in Somersville, Connecticut, a week later. They married in 1927 and had two children, Howard and Alice Katherine. They purchased the Tolson house in 1937 without ever having seen the inside, and by the summer of 1942, Theodore had a summer job with the T.A. Loving Company building Ammunition Dump Road. In 1948, Theodore became principal and Alice one of the four teachers at Ocracoke School, where they remained for 14 years. Alice enjoyed gathering island information, publishing articles in the school paper and in an Outer Banks newspaper. Theodore was a mediator, often settling disputes and offering marital counseling. Theodore died in 1956 and Alice in 1977, and they are both buried in the Ocracoke Community Cemetery. (OPS.)

Eight

LESSONS LEARNED AND HYMNS SUNG

In *A Blessed Life: Growing Up on Ocracoke Island*, Della Gaskill recalls, "The old school house was a beautiful building, but they tore it down for which we are very sorry. . . . We had teachers that really taught us, and we learned from those teachers. . . . They were excellent teachers. My first grade teacher was Miss Lela Howard, and she was the best teacher that I had during my schooldays." Pictured is an elementary class in 1927. (Vince O'Neal.)

The first school on Ocracoke was located at the Hatteras Inlet Station and was called Captain Wilson's School. In the village, due to the good-natured rivalry between the Creekers and the Pointers, two schools emerged. The Creekers' school was located in the front of Nathaniel Jackson's house, and the Pointers' school was to the left of James Garrish Jr.'s house. The lodge was the next school on the island. It was held in the middle section of what is today the Island Inn and included grades one through seven. A Mrs. Lacie taught there in 1907, Sofia Williams and Stanley Wahab in 1910, and Clifton Wahab in 1914. During this time, a private school was held in the Rondthaler home by Laura Smith, who taught primary through seventh grades. Those who wanted to further their education had to go off-island. In 1917, the new and combined Ocracoke School was built near its present-day location next to the Methodist church. (OPS.)

The 1917 Ocracoke School was a one-story structure divided into six rooms, and each room had its own entrance. The library had a potbellied stove. The classrooms were multigrade, with one teacher per classroom and approximately three to eight students per class. No cafeteria was built, since the children went home for lunch, a practice that still exists today. (OPS.)

The first high school graduating class of 1931 had three students—Russell Williams, Mable Fulcher, and Lucy Garrish. Before that, some families sent their high school students to the Washington Collegiate Institute in Washington, North Carolina, or to Hatteras. This photograph shows the graduating class of 1950: from left to right, Maude Ellen Garrish (Ballance), Hazel Wahab (Garrish), Wanda Simpson (Robinson), Mickey Garrish (O'Neal), Peggy Spencer (O'Neal), and Audrey O'Neal (Lynn). (Chester Lynn.)

A recreation hall was added behind the school using barracks from the naval base. In 1971, the school building was razed to make room for the new modern-style structure that exists today. Although the new school's style was disliked by many Ocracokers, a new gymnasium, multipurpose room, and an elementary wing were added. Today, the school houses prekindergarten through 12th grade with between 170 and 180 students. (OPS.)

Sports play an important role in island life. Before organized sports, students used to entertain themselves with cat, a form of colonial baseball that remained popular on the island long after it had died out elsewhere. Pictured from left to right, Jimmy Spencer, Walter C. O'Neal, Ikey D. O'Neal, Sigma Willis, Ward Garrish, Johnny Midgett, Cantwell Howard, Larry Simpson, and Elmer Midgett are playing the popular game. (OPS.)

Ocracoke School is a unique and special place. There is no bus service, so many teachers and students walk or bike to school, students either go home for lunch or bring a packed lunch, and teachers are traditionally called by their first names. In *Ocracokers*, Alton Ballance, a native of Ocracoke and a past teacher at the school, quotes former teacher Lynn VanOrsdale: "The real Ocracoke is so much more than what people see on a fast summer trip. Attachments here run deep. In our school before you even realize it, these kids have crawled into your soul." Above is Ocracoke School in the 1940s, when the Navy base was on the island. Below is the new structure, completed in 1971. (Above, OBHC; below, OPS.)

The Methodist church has always been a part of Ocracoke culture. The earliest historical record of a congregation on Ocracoke is from 1828, when the Methodist Episcopal church was created. The Reverend J. Atkinson was pastor. A conflict occurred between members of the church, tearing it into two factions. Island history has it that this was due to some members not wanting to learn how to read music notes and purchase new hymnals. Thus, the Northern Methodist Church, which favored the reading of musical notes, split from the Southern Methodist Church, which was seen as the original church. In 1883, the Wesley Chapel, pictured here, was built on the present-day Back Road and housed the Northern Methodist Church. The original Southern Methodist Church was located on Howard Street and from 1869 to 1937 was never without a pastor. (OPS.)

The Methodist churches joined together in 1939. The Reverend E.C. Cowan was appointed pastor. The new church building, still in use today, was dedicated on July 4, 1943, with Rev. William Dixon as pastor. Lumber from both the Northern and Southern churches was used to build the new church, and members from both congregations shared in construction. (OPS.)

Homer Howard constructed the cross that sits on the altar of the Methodist church. The cross was built out of salvaged wood from the ship *Caribsea*, which was sunk by a U-boat on March 11, 1942. Aboard that ship was Jim Baum Gaskill, son of Pamlico Inn owners Capt. Bill and Annie Gaskill. Jim's license and nameplate also washed ashore near the inn. (Chester Lynn.)

In the late 1930s, members of the Pentecostal Holiness tradition visited Ocracoke and needed a place for their revivals. Elizabeth Styron provided her front yard and her enclosed porch on Lighthouse Road. She eventually donated the lot beside her home for an official church building in 1938. On May 2, 1947, the church became an Assembly of God affiliate. With a separate parsonage beside the church, buildings were added in 1948 from the dismantled Navy Base and attached to the back of the church to be used as Sunday school rooms. On November 3, 1954, fire broke out in the parsonage, and the building was destroyed. The original Assembly of God church was moved to its present-day location on Highway 12 and is now used as a rental cottage. A new Assembly of God church was built. (Both, OPS.)

Nine

UNCLE SAM
COMES A-CALLING

The battle over the East Coast began after Hitler declared war on the United States, as he wanted to cut off the United States' ability to ship goods up and down the coast. Ocracoke stood right in this path. By 1942, there were six to eight U-boats off of North Carolina. Island residents felt their homes shake and saw torpedoed ships burning. Soon, debris and bodies began washing ashore. (OPS.)

The federal government bought land at the southern end of Ocracoke for the Navy base near today's decommissioned Coast Guard station. A medical facility, administrative offices, a commissary, an officers' club, a training field, and three power plants were constructed. The administrative building had sleeping quarters for 400 as well as a mess hall for 1,500. The US Navy hospital, pictured below, had 30 beds and was located where the Scott house had been. The government also leased 47 acres for an ammunition dump and installed a detection system for finding German subs in an area called Loop Shack. (Both, OPS.)

During World War II, U-boats attacked 400 tankers, freighters, and passenger ships, killing 5,000 people. Eighty-seven ships were sunk off the Outer Banks, turning the area into "Torpedo Junction." Islanders were aware of the danger, seeing and hearing explosions off the shore. During the first six months of 1942, six ships were sunk off of Ocracoke. On March 26, 1942, the *Dixie Arrow* was hit. The tanker was carrying 96,000 barrels of Texas crude oil. The torpedo set off an explosion killing 11 of the 33 crew members. The final ships to be sunk by U-boats in 1942 were the tanker *F.W. Abrams* on June 19 and the cargo ship *Nordal* on June 24. (Both, OPS.)

The building with the stack is the incinerator. The other buildings are training quarters for enlisted men. After the Navy left, some of these cottages were moved to Parkers Creek and used as a hunting and fishing camp. After the land was turned into National Park Service property, these cottages were once again moved. The Gaskill family turned them into the Wagon Wheel cottages. (OPS.)

The Navy base included an engineering building and a movie theater. According to Della Gaskill, the building remained long after the base had been dismantled: "After they left, it stayed for a lot of years. Kermit Robinson used it . . . to repair vehicles in, and he kept it open to use so that you could drive on the dock and get to the building." (OPS.)

Because of the base's location, homeowners such as Thadeas Scarborough, Charlie Scarborough, and George O'Neal were forced to evacuate their homes. Pictured is George and Annie Belle O'Neal's home. According to Chester Lynn, his grandparents tried to fight the loss of their home, but to no avail. Just minutes after being handed the check, Annie Belle returned for her belongings, only to find dynamite already on the porch. (Chester Lynn.)

Taken from the naval base, this photograph shows the remains of a twin-engine bomber that crashed near Ocracoke. While attempting to land on the mainland, the plane ran out of gas and crashed into Pamlico Sound. All of the crew except for the pilot bailed out of the plane before the crash. The pilot was found in the cockpit. (OPS.)

At the start of the war, the US Navy did not have an adequate number of warships to battle the U-boats. Instead, it used local sailboats and private yachts. It called this the "Hooligan Fleet." It was soon discovered that these small ships were no match for German submarines. They were instead used in search-and-rescue operations. (OPS.)

Silver Lake was dredged during World War II to allow the larger Navy vessels to pass, as seen here. The two streams that separated the island, the Big Gut and the Little Gut, were filled in using the dredged sand. One 135-foot-long wooden pier was constructed with a fueling station. The Coast Guard docked 18 vessels and the Navy 8 to 10. (OPS.)

On the outskirts of the village, on the ocean side, was an area known as Loop Shack Hill. It housed two top secret towers for the US Navy that watched German submarine activity—a radar and a lookout tower. When the U-boats were defeated, the Navy base became the advanced amphibious training facility for a special forces group in late 1943. The "Beach Jumpers" were the forerunners to the Navy SEALs. According to Lt. Jack Carlton, Ocracoke's "isolation was for secrecy and the secrecy was extended to us. We didn't really know what we were up to until we got overseas." A monument on Ocracoke was dedicated to the Beach Jumpers on Friday, October 23, 2009, near Loop Shack Hill. Members of the Beach Jumper Association attended. Ocracoke local historian Earl O'Neal was instrumental in procuring this memorial. (Both, OPS.)

The Navy paved the first road on Ocracoke Island in 1942; it would become known as Ammunition Dump Road. At the end of this concrete road, the Navy stored live ammunition in bunkers. The concrete bunkers were piled with sand so that they could not be discernable from the air. After the Navy base was abandoned, so were the bunkers, which were often explored by island children. Ocracokers still refer to this road as Ammunition Dump Road, although today it is named Sunset Drive. Street signs and names were not officially part of the Ocracoke landscape until 1999. (Both, OPS.)

Aycock Brown was a civilian investigator with the Office of Naval Intelligence during World War II. From Happy Valley, North Carolina, Brown visited Ocracoke in the 1920s after being offered a free vacation by Capt. Bill Gaskill in exchange for promoting the island. While visiting, Brown found his bride, Esther Styron. During the war, Brown's job was to identify bodies from torpedoed ships and interview survivors. In 1951, Brown became the director of the Dare County Tourist Bureau, and he is largely responsible for the tourism boom. "An Outer Banks legend: How one man turned obscure barrier beaches into an international tourist destination," an article by Lorraine Eaton in the May 30, 2016, *Virginian-Pilot*, cites a 1974 interview Brown had with historian David Stick in which Brown comments that Ocracoke locals "used to think I was a great guy because I had a typewriter." In the 1920s, thousands of people visited the Outer Banks; in the 1950s, tens of thousands came; by the time Brown retired, millions of people toured the area. Philip Howard notes in the entry titled "Aycock Brown," in the July 11, 2016, *Ocracoke Island Journal*, that just before his death in 1984, Brown lamented his impact on tourism, saying he was "worried about what he had done." Many of his photographs have been used in this book. (OBHC.)

Aycock Brown traveled in the spring of 1942 to Morehead City, where he met Lt. Thomas Cunningham. Brown asked Cunningham for flags to place on the caskets of British soldiers. Lieutenant Cunningham gave him six Union Jacks. Also that spring, Wahab Howard, the chief of the Ocracoke Navy Base, met Lieutenant Cunningham at a restaurant in Norfolk. On May 11, 1942, a U-boat hit the British trawler HMT *Bedfordshire* off Cape Lookout. All the crew was lost. On May 14, two bodies washed up on Ocracoke's shore and were discovered by Coastguardsman Arnold Tolson of Hatteras. Brown was called to investigate. He recognized the body of Lieutenant Cunningham. Howard confirmed the identification. The other was Telegraphist Stanley R. Craig. The men were buried on a plot of land donated by the family of Capt. David Williams. Brown draped the two Union Jacks he had remaining over the caskets of Lieutenant Cunningham and Stanley Craig. A week later, two other bodies were discovered. (OPS.)

North Carolina leased 2,290 square feet of land to England for the British Cemetery. Each May since the sinking of the *Bedfordshire*, members of the US Coast Guard, the National Park Service, and the Royal Navy gather to honor the fallen British soldiers, ending with the traditional 21-gun salute. In 1970, the British ambassador presented a wreath during the event. In 2012, Lieutenant Cunningham's son, who was born after his father's death, attended the ceremony. The plaque on the graveyard reads, " 'If I should die, think only this of me; that there's some corner of a foreign field that is forever England . . . ' Robert Brook 1867–1915." (Both, OPS.)

On September 14, 1944, a hurricane ravaged Ocracoke. The winds blew in excess of 100 miles per hour, with tides at 14 feet. Six homes were demolished, as was the Pamlico Inn, pictured here. In her book *A Blessed Life: Growing Up on Ocracoke Island*, native islander Della Gaskill calls the hurricane of 1944 one of the "worst storms we ever had." (OPS.)

A description of the hurricane of 1944 was written on the wall of this home, known as the Hurricane House. It lists hour-by-hour details of what occurred during the storm. The 7:30 a.m. entry states, "Island completely under water. Most fishing boats blown far ashore, causing considerable damage to boats and docks. Mailboat tossed ashore close to coffee shop [Island Inn]. Six houses completely demolished. . . . No lives lost." (OPS.)

Ten

PONIES AND FIGS

Approximately 300 cattle and 400 Banker ponies roamed free on the island in the early 1900s. By the 1940s, only the Banker ponies and 200 cattle remained. By that time, Ocracoke could not butcher its own meat because of regulations set forth by the US government. With advent of the National Park Service, all free-roaming livestock was banned, and in 1959 the present-day pony enclosure was built. (OBHC.)

Many theories exist about how and when the horses first appeared on the island. One is that they came from Sir Richard Grenville's ship, the *Tiger*, which ran aground near the Ocracoke Inlet in 1585. Another is that Spanish ships from the Caribbean, making their way along the Gulf Stream to Hatteras, might be responsible for the herd. (SANC.)

Horses have been documented on Ocracoke since the 1730s. Settlers used them to pull carts. The Life-Saving Service used them in beach patrols. Sometimes, ponies stampeded through the village. Banker ponies, which are technically horses, are smaller than most. They have a unique shape, posture, and color. They have five lumbar vertebrae instead of six and 17 ribs instead of 18. (OPS.)

However they arrived, the horses are a source of history and pride on the island. Pony roundups were a major event held on July 3 and 4. The pennings began on the 3rd as everyone corralled the horses from all around the island. In the early 1900s, there were five herds taken to the area near today's Coast Guard station, Horse Pen Point. In later years, they were corralled to Island Inn and then to Berkley Manor. The last area used is the site of today's pony pen. Once corralled, foals were branded or sold. The ponies were held in the pen for just a few hours before being released. (Both, OBHC.)

Ocracoke Troop 290 was the only mounted Boy Scout troop in the country. Marvin Howard was the Scoutmaster. Each member had to catch and tame a horse and was often followed by a black-and-white dog named Tippy. The troop is featured in a *Boys' Life* magazine article and is part of a story in the 1959 children's novel *Wild Pony Island*, by Steven W. Meader. As well as participating in the July penning, the mounted Boy Scouts also marched in parades and participated in races. Members of the troop pictured below in the mid-1950s are, from left to right, (front) Ronnie Van O'Neal, Billy Garrish, James Barrie Gaskill, Jack Wilson, Wayne Teeter, and Stanley Gaskins; (back) Joe Ben Garrish, David Esham, Rudy Austin, Lindsey Howard, and Edward Carlson O'Neal. (Both, OPS.)

Troop members indicated that it was often difficult for the horses they caught to get acclimated to eating oats rather than salt and beach grasses. Indeed, the ponies and other roaming livestock readily grazed upon the natural vegetation on the island, which led to erosion. In 1957, the state legislature passed a bill that required the Banker ponies and other livestock to be permanently penned. Since the 1960s, the National Park Service has cared for the wild ponies. There are less than 20 horses in the Ocracoke herd today. The latest addition was Jobelle, born in the spring of 2017. (Both, OPS.)

Having the ponies roam the island was a way of life for Ocracokers. Here, Marie Eley is spoiling a Banker pony with a treat. Alex and Marie Eley opened the Pony Island Motel and Restaurant. The Esham family purchased the motel in 1973, and it is currently owned by David Scott and Melinda Esham. The restaurant is owned by Vince and Sue O'Neal. (Vince O'Neal.)

In the 1970s, the Ocracoke herd was close to extinction. In November 1974, Jim Henning was transferred from Bodie Island to Ocracoke to become the district ranger. Jim and his wife, Jeanetta, nurtured the ponies back to a larger herd. Jim, with the help of residents and nationwide veterinarians, trained the horses for mounted beach patrol, and he started a living history program. (OPS.)

Even in the early 1900s, Ocracokers reveled in the festivities of Independence Day. The July 6, 1914, *Wilmington Morning Star* reports that Ocracoke's Fourth of July celebration included a pony penning, a motorboat race, and an auction sale. By the 1920s, a parade had been added that involved decorating elaborate floats for competitions. Annie Belle Fulcher O'Neal is pictured dressed in men's hunting clothes sitting beside her husband, George F. O'Neal, ready for the parade. In the 1950s, Sam K. Williams, Willie Hunnings, Charlie Garrish, and Owen Gaskill cavorted on a music-inspired float. In 1953, Alice Rondthaler wrote that a flag-raising ceremony was added to the day's schedule. Both the parade and flag-raising are events still enjoyed today. (Right, Chester Lynn; below, OPS.)

Figs were brought to Ocracoke Island in the 1700s by the colonists. Five varieties date back to the 18th century: the pound fig, the sugar fig, the white fig, the brown turkey fig, and a greenish fig from Portsmouth. This image from the early 1900s shows a large fig tree behind Annie Belle (left) and her friend Malsey. Today, there is an annual Ocracoke Fig Festival. (Chester Lynn.)

Yaupon, a species of holly, grows wild on Ocracoke. While Native Americans were the first to discover its use, islanders traditionally dried the yaupon's leaves to make tea. Sisters Mildred (pictured below with an unidentified child) and Muse Bryant gathered yaupon with their grandmother, Winnie Blount. Mildred, born in 1907 to Leonard and Jane Bryant, moved off-island in 1929 but returned in 1943 to work for Carlton Kelly. (OPS.)

Ocracoke brogue is the distinctive dialect spoken by locals. Extensively studied by Prof. Walt Wolfman of North Carolina State University, the brogue has many unique qualities. One distinction is the substitution of an "oi" for the long *i* sound. So "high tide" is pronounced "hoi toide." Different vocabulary words are used, such as "buck" for friend and "mommicked" for teased. Because of Ocracoke's isolation, the brogue has survived for over 250 years. "Although our dialect and accent have been the subject of much interest over the last century or so, I won't try to explain them. Maybe our speech does have traces of Elizabethan English, as some historians claim. . . . Any community which has experienced few outside influences is likely to keep the speech of its first settlers," says Alton Ballance in *Ocracokers*. (OBHC.)

Ocracoke is rich in history, and its people are proud of their culture and traditions. Local historian Philip Howard commented on his blog, "One of the reasons I personally collect island stories, and share them whenever the opportunity arises . . . is not only to hold on to a bit of the sense of shared history and culture that binds us together as a community, but also to encourage others to do the same." Ocracokers have experienced tragedies and celebrated triumphs together. Hardworking and devoted, the men and women of Ocracoke have lived their lives with dignity. The beauty of Ocracoke Island and the simplicity of its people can be summed up in Mariah Styron Bragg's burial marker: "She hath done what she could." (OBHC.)

BIBLIOGRAPHY

Ballance, Alton. *Ocracokers*. Chapel Hill: University of North Carolina Press, 1989.

Bragg, Cecil S. *Ocracoke Island: Pearl of the Outer Banks*. Manteo, NC: Times Print Co., 1973.

Dudley, Jack. *Ocracoke Album*. Morehead City, NC: Jack Dudley, 2005.

Fordon, Ruth and Jenny Scarborough. Ocracoke Walking Tour and Guide Book. Manteo, NC: Narayana, Inc., 2009.

Gaskill, Della. *A Blessed Life: Growing Up on Ocracoke Island*. Ocracoke, NC: self-published, 2013.

Goerch, Carl. *Ocracoke*. Winston-Salem: John F. Blair, 1956.

Howard, Philip. *Ocracoke Island Journal*. villagecraftsmen.blogspot.com.

———. *Village Craftsmen*. villagecraftsmen.com/ocracoke-newsletter.

McAllister, Ray. *Ocracoke: The Pearl of the Outer Banks*. Richmond: Beach Glass Books, 2016.

O'Neal, Calvin J., Alice Rondthaler, and Anita Fletcher. *The Story of Ocracoke Island: A Hyde County Bicentennial Project*. Charlotte: Herb Eaton, Inc., 1976.

O'Neal, Earl W. Jr. *Howards, Garrishes, Jacksons, and Stowes of Ocracoke Island, North Carolina: Their Ancestors and Descendants*. Ocracoke, NC: self-published, 2007.

———. *O'Neals of Ocracoke Island: Their Ancestors and Descendants*. 2nd ed. Ocracoke, NC: self-published, 1999.

DISCOVER THOUSANDS OF LOCAL HISTORY BOOKS FEATURING MILLIONS OF VINTAGE IMAGES

Arcadia Publishing, the leading local history publisher in the United States, is committed to making history accessible and meaningful through publishing books that celebrate and preserve the heritage of America's people and places.

Find more books like this at
www.arcadiapublishing.com

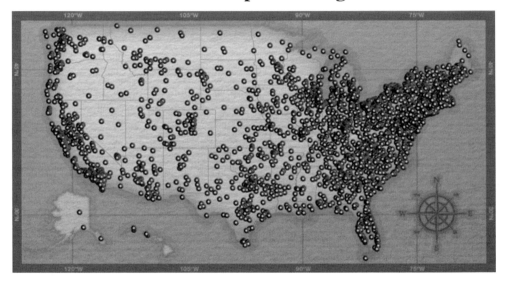

Search for your hometown history, your old stomping grounds, and even your favorite sports team.